10/03

Phaidon Press Limited
Regent's Wharf
All Saints Street
London N1 9PA

First published 1996
© 1996 Phaidon Press Limited
This edition first published 2000
© 2000 Phaidon Press Limited

ISBN 0 7148 3999 X

A CIP catalogue record for
this book is available from
the British Library

Printed in China

The Colours of Light | Tadao Ando Architecture | Richard Pare Photography | Tom Heneghan Introduction

# Contents

Richard Pare travels the world photographing objects – cities, gardens and architecture. Guided by his own sensitivity, he projects them into unique photographic landscapes. Egypt, Russia and Japan, in particular, are places that Pare has returned to many times, finding things that have a continual attraction for him. While architectural photography is most commonly a medium of reportage, Pare's sense of beauty allows him to capture the drama of architecture. His work is an example of representation where details can grasp the essence of a building far more effectively than images of the whole. He discovers scenes in a building which even the architect has not noticed; he allows the materials to be self-explanatory and the forms to express their functions. The light coming into a space is frozen in an instant in Pare's viewfinder and printed on our retinae, becoming a phantasmic beauty beyond real time.

Tadao Ando

Architecture and Ethics

T adao Ando's buildings have been extensively published in international books and journals; still, their authentic qualities have remained difficult to sense through photographic illustration. Perhaps the fact that Richard Pare is a photographer of architecture rather than an architectural photographer explains both his approach to his work and the character of the images presented here. While other photographs have conveyed Ando's extraordinary facility for the sculpting of form and space, the sensitive experiential qualities and the surprising delicacy of his architecture have only been discerned by visitors to the actual projects. Pare's works overcome this limitation, and present us with an unexpected paradox; as Karl Schawelka writes: 'There are buildings that I believed I knew [from visits] until I saw the photographs of Richard Pare.'[1]

Pare photographed Ando's works during regular and lengthy visits to Japan between 1985 and 1993 – a period of considerable significance in the development of the architect's career. Including buildings in existence at the time of his first visit and those completed during the late months of 1993, Pare's portfolio represents a cross section of Ando's œuvre, allowing us to trace both the evolution and the consistency of the architect's thoughts and intentions.

Occasionally, Richard Pare has revisited Ando's buildings to confirm, in his words, the 'veracity' of his original 'interpretation' and, where he deemed necessary, to rephotograph in order to achieve more 'accuracy'. But Pare's photographs are not windows. Changing light and weather conditions inevitably alter our perception of any building minute -by-minute and the physical characteristics of film and print-paper restrict the reproduction of true depth and realistic colouration. Pare's usage of the word 'accuracy' implies more than factual documentation. Through his exclusively visual medium he attempts to

1
Karl Schawelka, *Richard Pare*,
(Gesamthochschule, Kassel University, 1992)

communicate the way Ando's buildings can be sensed or experienced, rather than as they are seen. Unlike most photographers, Pare prints all his own work, which allows him the opportunity to manipulate his final images. In his photographs of Ando's Forest of Tombs Museum, Kumamoto (1992), for example, he toned the concrete walls with a slight warming of the overall colour, seeking – through this enhanced pigmentation – to provide a rendering that captures the essence of the place as carried in his memory of a visit. In his photographs, Pare employs no unusual camera angles or distortions. His images are almost all as seen from eye-level – as experienced and as disclosed to visitors along the architect's *promenade architecturale*. In his framing, Richard Pare echoes the character of each building. The almost aggressive cut of his images of the Museum of Literature, Himeji (1991), reflect the power of the building's collision of overlapping geometries. The tranquil openness of his images of the Water Temple, on Awaji Island (1991), emphasize the serene beauty of this pond gently levitated above the brow of a hill. Pare seeks through his photographer's art to explain the art of the architect.

The continuing fascination that Pare has maintained with Ando's work during the many years that he has been preparing this portfolio, lies not only in the handsomeness of the building forms. There is evidently common ground between the spareness of Pare's aesthetic sense and that of Ando, but Pare's respect arises principally from his regard for the moral imperative or ethical motivation that frames Ando's philosophy, and which underlies and is expressed through all of Ando's works. It is an ethic of simplicity, of the individual versus collective society and – in a sociological rather than political sense – of society versus the state. Ando's work aims to reconnect man with man and man with nature, with architecture as the intermediary.

Though it inevitably adheres to the internal disciplines of its own culture, Ando insists that architecture must be more than an autonomous art form, and must concern itself primarily with the enrichment of the human spirit. The simplicity of such a proposition belies the extreme complexity of the concepts and concerns that frame the only superficial simplicity of his buildings. For an understanding of these issues it is necessary to consider the extraordinary, now legendary, Sumiyoshi Row House, Osaka (1976) – the touchstone to which Ando, and all critics, almost always return in any attempt to explain his approach. Through this minute building, occupying a site area of less than 60 square metres, Ando effectively declared his architectural manifesto.

At Sumiyoshi, tall concrete walls delineate the site boundaries, enfolding the inhabitants in their own world, within which they occupy spaces of almost monastic bareness, and are obliged to harmonize their daily lives with the vagaries of the climate, as they pass from room to room through the roofless court at the centre. As Ando explains, unlike Western cultures, where the 'world of man' and the 'natural world' are considered separate, Japanese society traditionally views both as continuous: 'According to the traditional Japanese interpretation, architecture is always one with nature, and it attempts to isolate and fix, at a point of time, nature as it exists in its organic metamorphoses. In other words, it is an architecture reduced to the extremes of simplicity, and an aesthetic so devoid of actuality and attributes that it approached theories of "mu", or "nothingness". Connections with nature are effected by subtle transformations caused in part by delicate contrasts of light and shade. In these connections it is the wall, made as light and thin as possible, that permits – or, more accurately, evokes – space.'[2] In the harshness of Sumiyoshi's metropolitan context, Ando internalized nature, which would in an earlier age

2
Kenneth Powell (ed), *Tadao Ando –
Buildings, Projects, Writings,* (New York,
Rizzoli International, 1984), p 142

have been found at the perimeter: 'The past ideal of being at one with nature is far removed from reality. Just as civilization and culture have been changing, so has nature … I think that in such an age, the relationship between man and nature must inevitably change. My goal has not been to commune with nature as-it-is, but rather to try to change the meaning of nature through architecture. The process has been one of rendering nature abstract through architecture … I would like man and nature to confront each other, and to have a tension maintained with regard to each other. I want to create a place where that will occur.'[3] Rain and shafts of sunlight penetrate the stillness and geometrical purity of the Sumiyoshi courtyard. Emphasized by the unchanging datum of the architecture, against which they are seen, these fluctuating natural elements acquire an actuality, which is diluted in the open expanse of the external world. While the windowless perimeter walls defiantly exclude the aridity of the encircling urban morass, their purpose is also to capture and emphatically include nature as an inextricable part of the inhabitants' life. As Ando explains his houses are 'devices for appropriating nature'.[4]

All Ando's works are characterized by this confrontation between nature and architecture. Nature is neither additional to his buildings, nor decorative – planting is rarely found in or around his buildings – but is for him a principal component: 'I believe that "architectural materials" are not limited to wood or concrete that have tangible forms, but go beyond to include light and wind – which appeal to our senses.'[5] Nature cuts deeply into both his architecture and into the lives of the inhabitants, forging a dialogue with both. His repeated use, in many works, of apertures between his walls and ceilings is not only for the architectural purpose of identifying the independence of the two planes, or to beautify the interior walls with patterns of falling light. Their essential purpose is to

3
Tadao Ando, *Space Design*,
September 1989, p 36

4
Powell (ed), *Tadao Ando*,
1984, p 25

5
Tadao Ando, *Space Design*,
June 1981, p 15

render the perfectly proportioned spaces fluid through the admission of nature. By measuring time and nature through the movement of shadows, or the sound of rain on the rooflights above, these apertures unite the life of the space itself with the lives of its human occupants.

Sumiyoshi, like all of Ando's subsequent houses, is not for the faint of heart. These are houses for those who identify with Ando's exasperation with the soullessness of a modern world, in which convenience is sought at the expense of spiritual richness, resulting, as he suggests, in a trivialization of human existence: 'it is important to discover what is essential to human life, and to consider what "abundance" truly means. An architectural space, stripped of all excess and composed simply from bare necessities, is "true" and convincing because it is appropriate and satisfying. Simplification through the elimination of all surface decorations, the employment of minimal, symmetrical compositions, and limited materials constitutes a challenge to contemporary civilization.'[6] In their plainness, Ando's buildings propose an alternative vision of life, and to understand correctly Ando's architecture, it is important to realize how sincerely he feels this to be his responsibility as an architect. We miss the point if we assess his work only on the level of its charismatic appearance. We must judge his simple forms and bare concrete surfaces not merely as his aesthetic preferences, but primarily as expressions of his underlying ethical position.

In a 1986 essay, Ando discussed the *shintai*, a word denoting the sentient being around whom his architecture is formed: 'Man is not a dualistic being in whom spirit and flesh are essentially distinct, but a living, corporeal being active in the world ... The world that appears to man's senses and the state of man's body [are] interdependent ... The body articulates the world. At the same time, the body is articulated by the world.'[7] In the

6
Powell (ed), *Tadao Ando*, 1984, pp 24–5

7
Tadao Ando, 'Architecture and Body', *Precis*, (New York, Rizzoli International, 1988)

*shintai* there is no distinction between mind, body and spirit. It is only through all the senses that architecture can be truly understood; and, as Ando adds, it is only by employing all the sensibilities of the *shintai* that true architecture can be created. It is this intention of Ando's that Pare accents through his photographs. Free from extraneous information, and rarely with the inclusion of other human figures, the viewer enters, alone, into Ando's world – perceiving the tactile materiality of the architecture, the framing and infusion of nature, the phrasing of our sequential experiences and the interaction of the whole with the viewer's own cultural background. As Ando says: 'My spaces are born not of intellectual operations, but of the emotions rooted in the desires of many different people ... my spaces transcend theory and appeal to the deepest spiritual levels. In other words, my spaces relate to fundamental aspects of humanity.'[8]

Unlike any other major architect of the present day, Ando is an autodidact who has educated himself empirically by travelling internationally through many different cultures, his observations being informed by his innate sensitivity to three-dimensional space. However, the most powerful influence on his work has remained the traditional architecture of his own country – not the physical characteristics of this architecture, his work makes no reference to traditional forms or styles, but the ethereal aspects whereby light and shade, time and season, are the principal components of the user's experience. Ando's architectural vocabulary clearly derives from the compositional methods of European Modernism – his ideologies share much with those underlying the early days of that movement, and with those expressed by the traditional Sukiya architecture of his homeland. In the refined simplicity of their return to basics, both of these 'styles' reflected their creators' beliefs that social change can be effected or encouraged through the

8
Powell (ed), *Tadao Ando*,
1984, p 134

medium of architecture. But, despite these precedents, which Ando acknowledges, his work is neither a linear descendant nor a synthesis of these legacies. Instead, it can be seen formally and philosophically as a counter-proposal to both traditions. Against the randomness of Sukiya he proposes order, against the order of Modernism he proposes randomness. In contrast to the informal and additive planning of Sukiya, which directed space out from man towards the exterior landscape, Ando composes his buildings as geometric volumes that centralize space around the inhabitant, and their harmony or proportion relates them to man in the classical sense. Against the rationalism of Modernism, with its search for universal solutions and the primacy that it gave to theory, Ando introduces irrationality to reflect the unpredictability of human life. After locating the basic functions within his overall geometric order, he then opens – often between or at the overlap between functional zones – interstitial spaces which may, or may not, have implied use, but which accommodate the atypical aspects of everyday life that the Modernists failed to acknowledge. These interstitial spaces, by their existence, invite the inhabitant or user to determine their use, and to become a participant rather than merely an occupant of functionally prescribed zones.

Against his criticisms of Modernism's systematization, the consistency of Ando's architectural vocabulary might seem incongruous. From his earliest houses, to the many museums and international projects which are among his most recent body of work, Tadao Ando's buildings share a consistency of material, detailing and often virtually identical elements. But while the parts may be scarcely distinguishable, his buildings, when experienced, are each found to be singular, with no more than a kindred relationship. In each case his elements are inflected to their different uses, sites and surroundings, producing buildings that are individual, yet related in their manipulation of consistent issues. By limiting his palette of elements, he releases his imagination and inventiveness to encompass wider issues than mere formal play.

Ando's architecture is not to be found in physical material alone. Koji Taki offers an explanation of the eloquence Ando achieves through the superficial monotonality of his medium: 'In Japan, meaning is produced not through abrupt changes but through subtle variations …The sensory world which Ando is striving so hard to create is more a world of monotonality than a world rich in formal changes such as that pursued by other architects … [in Ando's work] can be seen that quality of Japanese monotonality which, through subtle change, can give rise to meaning.'[9]

The principal tangible component of Ando's architecture is the wall. As a 'territorial delineator' in his houses, it both separates and conjoins inhabitant and surroundings. Standing independent, as at the Children's Museum, Himeji (1989), it scythes through the landscape, emphasizing the natural topography by comparison with its man-made self. Masao Furuyama has written a perceptive study, analysing Ando's walls in terms of the classical orders – Tuscan walls, Doric, Ionic and Corinthian walls.[10] He explains that this ordering relates more to the sense of each wall in its context than to its particular physicality – with the exception of the Matsumoto House, Ashiya, Hyogo (1977), the material qualities of Ando's walls have been subject to little variation. Furuyama evokes Ando's concern with the loss of meaning in modern architecture. Discussing the symbolism in traditional Japanese architecture of the single non-structural post and the symbolism of the colonnade in the West, Ando writes: 'The development of the modern rigid-frame liberated architectural spaces [structurally], but in giving precedence to function it underplayed the significance of

9
Koji Taki , 'Tadao Ando',
ed Powell, Tadao Ando,
1984, p 22

10
Masao Furuyama, Space Design,
September 1989, p 169

the post. The rigid-frame system … has robbed the post of its myths and the colonnade of its rhythm. Under such circumstances, the wall emerges as a major theme.'[11]

The intensity of meaning embodied in Ando's walls is, perhaps paradoxically, due to their abstinence from customary means of architectural expression. In their absolute plainness, they deny symbolism. They are mute, and it is in this very silence that their expressiveness lies. Of dimensions that generally exceed those required for utilitarian structural purposes – they often stand alone without load-bearing requirement or functional purpose – these walls insist on their individuality and suggest a brooding inner purpose. Unadorned, they proclaim their honesty and integrity. 'At a time when walls have begun to resemble paintings,' writes Furuyama, 'Ando's walls look askance at the prevailing trends [in architecture] … What makes Ando's walls different is their function in restraining the privileged status of the visual that has been taken for granted since the beginning of Modernism.'[12] In their absence of visual expression, Ando's walls can be understood as much through the body as by the eye. It is by contrast with their strength and permanence that we sense our own fragility.

Ando's walls have an ambiguous materiality, appearing both inorganic and organic. Meticulously crafted, and generally lacquered with a protective coating, the luminous sheen of their surfaces contradicts their mass, giving them a strangely ethereal and translucent delicacy. 'The concrete which I use does not give the impression of solidity or weight. My concrete forms a surface which is homogeneous and light … the surface of the wall becomes abstract; it is transformed into nothing and approaches infinity. The existence of the wall as a substance disappears. The only thing which remains for one's perception is the delineation of space.'[13]

11
Powell (ed), *Tadao Ando*,
1984, p 128

12
Masao Furuyama, *Space Design*,
September 1989, p 170

13
Tadao Ando, 'Rokko Housing',
*Quaderini di Casabella*, 1986, p 62

Fabricated generally from the hardest of materials – concrete, steel and glass – Ando's buildings can appear severe, yet at the same time, surprisingly gentle. While insisting on the highest quality of workmanship in the casting of his pristine walls, he makes no attempt to conceal the marks of successive concrete pours or the patching of imperfections, these being the natural characteristics of its fabrication. While Ando defines space by the abstract surfaces of his concrete planes, he views the material itself not as an abstract substance, but as an everyday material, which shows the skill of the craftsmen who form it. The traces of the mason, the welder and the concrete-worker are part of his overall concept for his architecture, through which he has said he seeks to reveal signs of life. In his use of facing stonework at Old/New Rokko Restaurant, Kobe (1986), and at Naoshima Contemporary Art Museum (1992), Ando employs texture not only for reasons of aesthetics or tactility, but also, sometimes almost subliminally, to impart meaning. The granite wall at Old/New mediates texturally between the nature of the trees it encloses and the plain abstractness of the concrete and steel, while it also recalls the traditional use of this material in residences of this area. The ochre rubble walls and paving stones at Naoshima harmonize with both the colour and the grain of the landscape, and emphasize the conceptual unity of the building with the promontory into which the museum has been excavated.

Reflecting on the time he spent during his childhood in a wood workshop opposite his family home, Ando recalls: 'I became interested in trying to make shapes out of wood. Just as people have individual personalities and facial appearances, so woods all have their own characteristics … I gained direct physical knowledge of the personalities of woods, their fragrances, and their textures. I came to understand the absolute balance between a form and the material it is made of … I experienced the inner struggle inherent in the human act of applying will to give birth to a form. In addition, my flesh came to know that creating something – that is, expressing meaning through a physical object – is not easy.'[14] This same concern with texture has informed all his subsequent works. In his architecture, sensuality is found not only in the materials or surface, but also in the textures of column against wall, curve against plane, light against shade and resonant sound against muted sound; the texture of time, the texture of history and the texture of space – all of which, undistracted by the economy of his forms, we are induced to experience.

In his photograph of the staircase at Kidosaki House, Tokyo (1986), Pare elucidates the complexities of Ando's textural finesse. An enclosed slate-covered stair ascends outside the line of an exterior wall, re-entering the house at a landing bounded by a curved glass wall and minimally detailed, steel handrail. While the steel echoes the precision of the glass, and its colour harmonizes with the slate floor, the grain of the slate echoes the surface of the concrete wall. The board-marked concrete and the wooden floor maintain an inevitable dialogue, while the colour of the latter engages with the colours of the tree seen diffused through the frosted glass. In its transmission through the glass, this nature is architecturalized, becoming as much an internal as an external element, with the changing colours of its seasonal transformations emphasized by its impassive architectural frame. In its translucency, the glass recalls traditional *shoji* paper screens, but in its curvature it is emphatically contemporary. The different textures of materials, colours, seasons, history and movement, and even the differential sound of footsteps on slate and oak, are all here captured in this deceptively simple photograph.

Ando has described how his architecture constantly oscillates between the polar extremes of: inside and outside; West and East; abstraction and representation; part and

14
Powell (ed), *Tadao Ando*,
1984, p 139

whole; history and the present; past and future; and simplicity and complexity.[15] Nature collides with the man-made, order with randomness, illogic with logic – the extremeness of one amplifying and accentuating its opposing partner. This collision of opposites is not an echo of the complexities of the modern world, but a response to the benumbed impoverishment of the spirit that this complexity induces. Against the discordancy of the commercial city, passivity and silence are not enough – his architecture is not an escape from the modern world, but a challenge to it. Through such oppositions, he has written: 'one might take Eastern and Western modes beyond their appearance of stable confrontation, to where their spatial sensibilities collide harshly, and a new place, resounding with potential, emerges'.[16] Ando has explained his aim in the projected Rokko Housing III, in Kobe, as the naturalization of architecture and the architecturalization of nature, suggesting that with this transformation the opposition between architecture and nature should vanish, and that, in the dialogue between the man-made and the natural, the boundaries of both will become dismantled. In the complex interlayering of their relationships, both will be recreated.[17] It is through the transfiguration of these antagonistic opposites – this dialogue of extremes – that Ando generates the lyricism, the originality and the meaning of his architecture.

In his collision of opposites, new spaces and new spatial meanings are bred. Through the many contradictions in his architecture, Ando seeks to create 'space of dynamic variance, space that pulsates in the gap between reality and fiction, between the rational and the illogical'.[18] He has described his architecture as 'realistic, while imbued with fiction', continuing, 'I neither undertake rational handling of architecture strictly in the realm of reality, nor attempt a "fabrication" whereby an architecture is solely infused with fiction.

15
Tadao Ando,
*Japan Architect*,
January 1991, p 13

16
Tadao Ando,
*El Croquis 44*,
September 1990, p 5

17
Tadao Ando,
'Rokko Housing 1,2,3',
*JA Library*, autumn 1993, p 148

18
Tadao Ando,
*El Croquis 44*,
September 1990, p 7

Rather, I want to instil fiction in the core of the real. Within a single architecture I seek to engage overwhelming fiction with reality, and to create de-familiarized space where fiction informs the everyday.'[19] Despite their solidity, his buildings often have the ethereal and fictional quality of dreams. While, in part, this derives from their translucent materiality and the perfect proportioning of the forms and the spaces they enclose, it arises more from Ando's unique methods of conceptual analysis.

As he writes: 'Perhaps it does not matter how pretty the details are, or how beautiful the finish is. What is important is the clarity of one's logic – that is, the clarity of the logic behind a composition … the quality that one recognizes through reason, not perception. What is important is "transparency" … the "transparency" of a consistent logic.'[20] Ando's is the logic of a singularly creative intelligence – a logic formulated by an insight which is, inevitably, not available to all. Of the open courtyard at the Sumiyoshi Row House, where one third of the tiny site is laid void, he writes: 'To enclose an outdoor space inside a building is contrary to common-sense … by the tenets of modern architecture this is preposterous and quite inconvenient.'[21] Yet, by the tenets of his own theories, such a move was both logical and essential. His dismissal of Modernism's obsessive emphasis on function, and his insertion within his buildings of indeterminate interstitial spaces, may, following the persuasiveness of his argument, be irrational while being simultaneously logical. Rationalism is conditional on which factors are included, or excluded, from the analysis, and what distinguishes Ando's transparent logic is that, rather than focusing on any limited set of issues, his overview is panoramic. He writes: 'I want to integrate, dynamically, two opposites – abstraction and representation. Abstraction is an aesthetic based on clarity of logic and concept, and representation is concerned with all historical,

19
Tadao Ando,
*El Croquis 44*,
September 1990, p 7

20
Tadao Ando,
*Japan Architect*,
January 1991, p 19

21
*Ibid* p 15

cultural, topographical, urban, and living conditions.'[22] While this intention is characteristic of all his works, in many of his recent projects he has seized the opportunity to amplify both aspects to such an intense level that our customary definitions and expectations of architecture are challenged.

The Chikatsu-Asuka Historical Museum of tumuli, Osaka (1994), rises as a stepped terrain, below which the exhibition spaces are located in a tomb-like chamber. Penetrating this diagonal plane, a tower of infinite darkness rises above the exhibition hall, chiming with an incised negative tower that frames the infinite light of the sky. Slashed across the staircase, a ramp leads between increasingly cavernous and echoing walls to the museum entrance, which is indented into the staircase to respect the location of adjacent tombs. The usual boundaries between architecture and conceptual art are breached. The visitor is engaged physically, perceptually and intellectually. And yet, no move is wilful. Despite the sculptural abstraction, each part has a logical functional purpose, and each part is inextricably related to the building's use and location. The stepped terrain serves as an arena for lectures, music and drama festivals, and for the contemplation of surrounding nature; externally, the positive tower forms a tall observation point overlooking the surrounding tombs; the negative tower admits daylight to the lowest exhibition floor level; and the ramp, although gently rising towards the entrance, is perceived as descending against the more steeply ascending plane of the staircase, evoking entrance into the depths of a tumulus, while its walls frame, at one end, views of the forest and, at the other, views of the lake. Arguably as much a land-form as a building, rarely does architecture approach such lyricism.

The Water Temple on Awaji Island is approached through the shade of trees, the composition presenting itself, at first, as only a long concrete wall cutting across a clearing.

22
*Ibid* p 14

Facing south, the glare from the wall is accentuated by sunlight reflecting upwards from white stones strewn at its base, producing a zone of ethereal illumination comparable to that of the translucent glazed corridor leading to the Chapel on Mount Rokko, Kobe (1986). Passing through the single opening in the Awaji wall, a second, curved wall leads visitors again from shadow into light towards the edge of the water-filled dish, which is the temple's horizontal, ever-changing and principal elevation, through which a staircase penetrates to the temple hall. Again, abstraction and representation overlap: the white stones clearly refer to those in the gardens of historical religious sites such as Ise shrine; waterlilies are the traditional symbol of the Shingon Buddhist sect that administers this temple; and Ando omits the massive roofs, which are customarily found on all Japanese temples, and in so doing disparages their authoritarian monumentality.

Similar in function to Chikatsu-Asuka, Ando's Forest of Tombs Museum, Kumamoto (1992) is, even more acutely, a building to observe from, rather than a building to observe. Two long walls are established, cutting out and defining a rectilinear slice of land, which is subdivided into four sequential courts. The first court, from which views are permitted only towards the forest, leads to a second, where the rear wall is temporarily omitted, allowing views out only towards adjacent farming land. A monumental staircase rises to an upper terrace, from which – for the first time – the ancient earth-mound tombs can be seen, and a long curved ramp descends to the museum itself, which is buried at subterranean level. Despite its extreme simplicity, this building develops an intensely complex relationship with its context. In a process of gradual disclosure, the building explains the history of the land and its culture. From the upper terrace, all the surrounding landscapes are viewed in juxtaposition and the allegorical meaning of the sequential courts can be understood. By emphasizing the forest, then farming, then the tombs, Ando explains the continuity of life in this district – the eternal forest, the tombs of the area's fifth-century rulers and its continuing agricultural economy. He writes: 'Architecture is the introduction of an autonomous object into the site but, at the same time … it is the discovery of the building that the site [itself] desires … The ways of life and customs of people from distant past to the future lie concealed there. Architecture is the act of discovering these things and bringing them to the surface.'[23] At Kumamoto, the surrounding landscape appears to implode into the building, while the building conceptually expands out to incorporate the entire surrounding landscape within its programme.

Such building types as temples and museums of tumuli might seem uniquely susceptible to such a meaningful, poetic approach, but powerful fictional space is also found in Ando's vast cylindrical glass-block atrium at the RAIKA Headquarters Building, Osaka (1989), realized within the prosaic programme of a commercial warehouse and office building, and in and around the stark concrete walls of his educational facilities at Himeji. Ando once said of his architecture: 'I try to please people with the unstained minds of children; very honest, very stainless – white'[24], and the commission for the Children's Museum, on a verdant landscape at Himeji, clearly offered an appropriate opportunity for a full pedagogical exposition of his ideas. In no way condescending, he refuses any kind of saccharine or whimsical expression, and lays before the growing minds of the children a complete and sophisticated vision of his alternative world. Walls reach out into nature, which is simultaneously emphasized and challenged by their precision, and by the geometry of the 'boxes' to which they are appended. The museum itself is reciprocally incised by nature – split into two volumes by a longitudinal gap, along which the volumes are

23
Tadao Ando,
*Japan Architect*,
January 1991, p 19

24
Tadao Ando, *Newsline*, vol 4, no 2
(New York, Columbia University,
Nov–Dec 1991), p 2

dislocated both vertically and horizontally – as if by the force of the terrain. A roofed, transverse void frames views towards the lake and landscape, and both openings draw the abstracted nature of sunlight, wind and rain deep into the centre of the complex. The whole building is surrounded by water cascades and pools, which can be seen as both architectural and natural elements, and which literally blur the edge between the building and the landscape. Indeed, the apparently abstract layout of the whole site is generated by a dialogue between geometry and landscape. Having identified locations for the two major buildings – the museum on a promontory and the workshop at an inlet – two straight paths and accompanying walls were laid along existing contour lines, with the intermediate plaza moderating both the change in level between the routes and their angle of incidence. A third wall, added at a matching angle, develops into the southern wall of the museum, geometrically fixing the orientation of the museum by an abstract reference to the topography of the adjacent landscape. It is in the intermediate plaza that Ando's approach is most clearly expressed. Sixteen concrete posts, each 9 metres high, define an implied cuboid, which confronts the randomness of the natural landscape by the logic of its geometry. The space between the posts measures the scale of the human figure, while the scale of the cuboid measures the scale of the surrounding landscape. At the same time it is devoid of purpose, it is a fictional place where the children may invent their dream-worlds. As he writes of the project: 'Not everything can be accounted for reasonably. I feel that the things which cannot be completely explained, or described in "fact", are valuable to architecture ... there are things in society that cannot be explained just in functional terms ... I have provided functionless columns and walls ... I feel this irrational quality is important. The modernism of the past became insipid because it rejected such irrationalism.'[25] In

25
Tadao Ando, *Japan Architect,*
January 1991, p 18

releasing his architecture from bondage to function, Ando has sought to liberate mankind from its equivalent enslavement.

Through Pare's images, the viewer will perceive the differences and similarities in the forms of Ando's earliest and more recent works. Achieving renown, initially, for his introspective, spartan and often low-budget urban residences – a building type with which he continues to be actively engaged – his principal buildings are now more often expansive and sculpturally expressive public museums, set within lush landscapes. Formal gestures, which in his smaller works were suppressed in order to give precedence to the dialogue between individual and internalized space, are now deployed, with surprising virtuosity, in animated dialogue with the openness of the surrounding external space. But while the scale, purpose and locations of his principal works have changed, his intentions have remained consistent. Houses, however widely publicized, are, by definition, for private experience, and although Ando has always concerned himself primarily with the individual, it is the individual as representative of all individuals. As he said of his earlier residential and commercial buildings, 'from the viewpoint of day-to-day relations with human beings, buildings of this kind represent the points from which architecture itself is generated'.[26] His works are each part of a continuing, evolving and cross-referential investigation of spatial prototypes, at all scales, through which he seeks ways to make physical his humanist ideologies.

While his works have become iconic in terms of twentieth-century architecture, Ando himself has remained an iconoclast. The urban guerrilla of the 1970s – standing resolute against the bourgeois world – is today still much in evidence. 'I believe that, however anachronistic it may sound, it is important to ask the fundamental question: "what is architecture?". The creation of architecture must be a criticism of the problems of today.

26
Powell (ed), *Tadao Ando*, 1984, p 138

It must resist existing conditions. It is only when one faces up to today's problems that one can really begin to deal with architecture.'[27] While his early and many of his recent houses clearly reproached and provoked society, in his larger public works his approach is more subtle, his methods having become more subversive with their increased sophistication. The open forums and stepped facades, which characterize so many of his recent buildings, are conceived as places of encounter – not only between people and nature, but also, in a country which is virtually devoid of public space in the Western sense, between people. Ando explains: 'Traditionally, in Japan, we do not have many plazas or public spaces, except the gardens of temples or shrines. During the 1960s and 70s there were many movements in Japan protesting against defence treaties, and the national authorities intentionally dismembered plazas and open spaces, and prohibited citizens gathering together to exchange opinions. If there are no public spaces, opinion is suppressed, and people are made into robots whose only purpose is to work. In the history of Western countries – for example at the time of the French Revolution – people struggled and fought to win democracy. But in Japan we have never had a serious struggle to gain democracy. Each of us, in our own way, must be conscious of this fact. Ever since I started, I have tried to express this struggle through my architecture. In my projects I try to create public spaces that will encourage dialogue. This might be an individual's dialogue between himself, nature, and time – or it might be a dialogue between people. I can't dictate how people will use these spaces, but I want them to be aware of the possibility of dialogue. Space cannot dictate to people, but it can guide people.'[28]

Ando has suggested that in terms of functional and technical requirements, architecture has – or can – overcome almost all difficulties.[29] But while acknowledging the

27
Tadao Ando, *El Croquis 44,*
September 1990, p 193

28
Interview between Tadao Ando
and the author, Osaka,
January 1993

29
Tadao Ando, *Newsline,* vol 4, no 2
(New York, Columbia University,
Nov–Dec 1991), p 2

importance of such factual or logical aspects, Ando believes that architecture has more essential responsibilities. For him, the creation of architecture must involve more than the production of commodities, however elegantly formed, and observing the tendency for architects to often concern themselves principally with the composition of spatial art, or to justify their works by the manipulation of abstruse theories, he insists that architecture must recover ways to re-connect with 'everyman' by interpreting, giving expression to, and often guiding, their fundamental aspirations.

In physical terms, the characteristics of Ando's buildings may be adequately, if not easily, replicated, and perhaps the true potency of his works can be judged by comparison of the originals with the many Ando-esque simulations that his influence has spawned throughout the world. In the works of his imitators we may find reminiscent forms and components, but the intelligence, the intensity and the sense of purpose are absent. In Ando we find a sculptor of exquisite forms, and a planner of extraordinary ingenuity, for whom neither form nor plan are of primary importance. While his works clearly demonstrate his preferences in these matters, these are merely aspects of his search to communicate with people's minds, and with their spirit. Through his architecture he enters into a dialogue with the user and visitor, offering – for their consideration – his view of the world. As he has written: 'If you cannot sense the "depth" or philosophy of the designer when you experience a building, the architecture is merely an economic activity ... [and] in that case, the architecture has little meaning for me.'[30]

30
Powell (ed), *Tadao Ando,*
1984, p 133

The Colours of Light

Atelier in Oyodo I

Atelier in Oyodo II

Noguchi House

Koshino House

Koshino House

# Kidosaki House

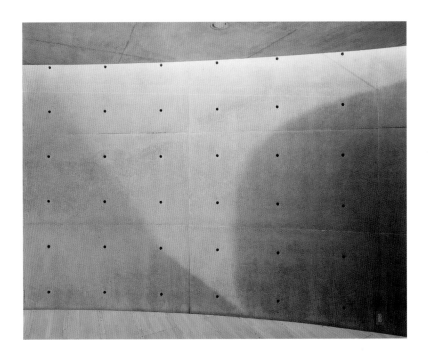

Collezione

Church of the Light

Tent Tea House

Hata House

Galleria Akka

Oxy Unagidani

Chapel on Mount Rokko

Old/New Rokko Restaurant

Children's Museum

RAIKA Headquarters Building

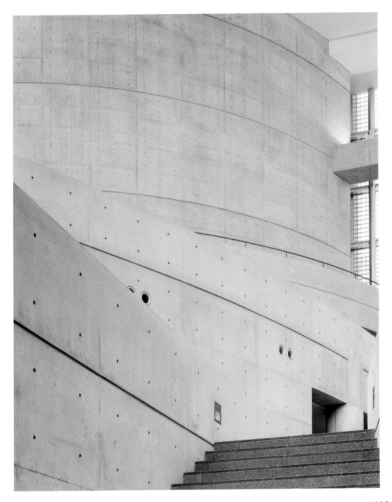

Museum of Literature

Church on the Water

Forest of Tombs Museum

Naoshima Contemporary Art Museum

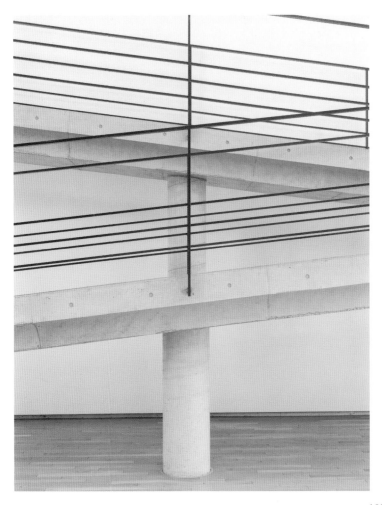

Rokko Housing II

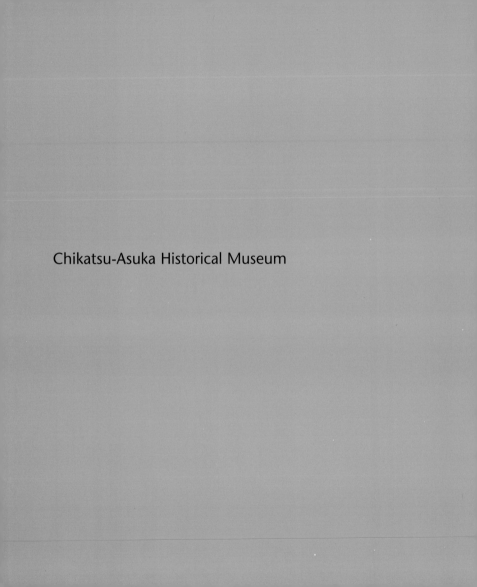

Chikatsu-Asuka Historical Museum

Vitra Seminar House

Water Temple

Nariwa Museum

Naoshima Contemporary Art Museum Annexe

FABRICA, Benetton Research Centre

Meditation Space, UNESCO

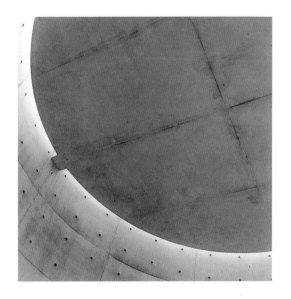

For Arabella and Rosamunde

'Time is the Movement of Eternity', *Plato*

T his book evolved from an auspicious meeting with Tadao Ando on my first visit to Japan in 1985. I already knew of Ando's architecture and took the opportunity while I was in the country to call the architect's office and arrange a visit. Thus began an investigation of the work that has enabled me to advance my ideas about the photographic representation of architecture. On that first occasion I photographed some seminal buildings. These included the Noguchi House, the Koshino House and some projects that had recently been completed. In the course of this first sojourn in Osaka I began to formulate the approach that has guided me in succeeding years, in my effort to comprehend the architectural endeavour.

As there was only a finite amount of time available on each journey, I worked in all weather conditions. This led to an awareness of the subtle effect that illumination has on Ando's architecture. Each structure became a succession of spaces in which the mass was dissolved in light, creating a heightened sense of the enclosed space. There was a remarkable afternoon of contemplation of light at the Water Temple on Awaji Island, where squalls of rain succeeded each other at the beginning of the rainy season. As the interior space of the temple is only dimly illuminated, it was necessary to leave the large camera exposing for long periods and there was plenty of time to observe the ephemeral effects of the light. Ascending from the hall of the temple to the exterior, I would find myself in a world that seemed different from the one I had visited only half an hour before. In recording what I saw again, I was able to recognize a myriad of subtle variations of colour and light. Each time I emerged, I tried to see more clearly what had altered in the qualities of space and light.

The photographs in this book take in the full range of Tadao Ando's work from the smallest structure, the Tent Tea House, one of three tea houses in Oyodo, to large-scale projects, such as the corporate headquarters for RAIKA at Osaka. Commercial buildings and private houses are included, as are the recent civic and institutional buildings, such as the Children's Museum at Himeji, and the most recently completed Chikatsu-Asuka Historical Museum in Osaka. I was able to survey the development of Ando's architectural thought from his earliest work to the projects in progress, which was present only in the form of models and drawings until the buildings were completed, while the book was in preparation. I returned to certain buildings after reflecting on the photographs from my previous visit, and when more than three years elapsed between visits, I found that my view of the work as a whole changed. These re-examinations either confirmed my previous conception of the building or I found that my view had changed radically. The intervening period amplified my understanding of the intention of the architect.

A photograph is a record of the present, but also a reflection of the tenets of photography. We carry an understanding of the historical canon forward to expand the potentials of photography for an interpretation of architecture based on the direct experience of the present. In photographing contemporary architecture a freedom of invention provides a sense of vitality and a contemporaneity. Photography can record and preserve the impressions of the completed work before the effects of time begin to leave accretions. The possibility of studying the architect's ideas from drawings, models and completed works leads to a broader range of photographic interpretations of architecture. Photography of architecture can present us with a possibility of seeing space independent of its function.

The space of the living world is filled with our activities. The space in a photograph is free of the multitude of phenomena. In seeing a photograph we become spectators unencumbered by the material conditions of existence.

Photography of architecture is an interpretation and a representation of the intrinsic elements of architecture: space, form, light and colour. The way light is directed is essential to the conception of space in architecture. Form, light and colour are inseparable and are simultaneous in space. All nature manifests itself by means of colour through the sense of sight. In nature space is continuous and infinite. A photograph of a landscape sets a momentary boundary to our field of vision. The exterior space of architecture has a coherence of structural form independent of its relation to its interior space and the surrounding environment. The interior space is composed of discontinuous and finite elements. Architectural drawings demonstrate the construction of space by adding plans and sections to elevations. However, the actual experience of moving within an interior space is indivisible and cannot be separated into these elements. Architecture is the processional arrangement and articulation of space. Photography strives to present a visual parallel to the experience of passing through architectural space by means of optical laws and the exactitude of presentation.

A photographic representation of architecture has a close affinity to a drawing and to the actual experience of space. The problem of rendering three dimensions in two dimensions does not arise for drawing and photography. In a drawing, the syntax is two dimensional and the semantics is three dimensional. In our reading of a drawing, lines, planes and angles refer to the corresponding three-dimensional elements, as elements of geometry correlate to physical space. As we know that a photograph is a direct record of the physical space of architecture, the two dimensionality of the image is read in dimensional terms. The conception of space in a drawing is static. Space itself is immovable. It has no movement, though all movement is in space. All space is actually static, and potentially dynamic. We conceive space statically, but we experience it dynamically. The space that is rendered in a photograph is a static space of potential movement.

In architecture, potential movement in space is indicated by light and shade. The representation of space in photography by means of light and shade is essentially different from pictorial representation in two ways: pictorial representations create an approximation or an illusion of actual space, and light is a derived effect sought out by means of colour; in photography, space and colour are unmediated. The observer recognizes the actual space and the colours as the objective correlatives of the photographic image. Light is primary both in the process and in the image of photography. When the illumination of the photograph is unmodified by supplemental lighting, we can see the way that the light falls naturally and the luminosity of the interior spaces. The observation of the seasons' cycles and changing illumination lead to an understanding of architectural forms in relation to the elements of nature.

The penetration of architectural space by the elemental aspects of natural phenomena – light, wind and the weather – is vital to the work of Ando. Ando's architecture has an outward image of clearly defined form. Often there is a dramatic display of brilliant sun and incisive shadow, falling across a subtly articulated space. The colouration of light seems each moment to be shifting and modifying the surrounding mass. It is this sense of dissolving mass in the constantly changing light that is a distinguishing characteristic of Ando's architecture. The concrete forms are imbued with a lightness that is in opposition to the considerable mass of the structure. We are in the presence of the weight of materials, but in immediate perceptual recognition there is no awareness of the overbearing mass which surrounds the observer. There is a sense of the revelation of space through luminous obscurity, that is most evident in the hall of the Water Temple.

In the architecture of Ando the harmony of form, light and colour is achieved through the synthesis of their inherently contrasting qualities. Light and colour, unlike the material elements of architecture are ephemeral and transient. The way light is modulated is central to Ando's architecture. A sense of serenity stems from the ways in which light and colour by their presence and absence provide articulation of form. There is a balance between tension and repose in the buildings, which produces both a calm and an invigorating effect. Ando's work is imbued with a deep sense of spirituality.

When we are in an architectural environment we see through the architect's eyes. There arises an empathy for forms in space. The idea of space we receive from a photograph derives from a contemplative perception of spatial relations. The task for the photographer of architecture extends beyond description or documentation of functional aspects. In a photograph it is possible to capture the ideas of space in architecture and show how the ideas are realized in the actual structure. Architectural space in each instance is determined by its relation to function. However, the conception of an individual space begins with an autonomy of form. There is no prescribed correlation between form and function. Form is timeless, while function is bound to the present. The validity of form transcends the utility of function. This apparent dichotomy is resolved by the quality that is inherent in all forms: universality. All particular functions are contained in the universality of form. Form is fluid in its relation to function: being engaged in the present, it continues to be accessible to future functions.

There is a parallel between the photographic representation of architecture and the performance of a musical score. Both architecture and music can be studied from infinitely different perspectives. Diverse approaches, which seek to establish a valid frame of reference, enhance our understanding of the work. Whether we stand before monuments of antiquity or contemporary architecture, the task of the photographer is the same: the exploration of the visual field leading to a discovery which enhances our knowledge of the visual world. Time in photography is always the eternal present, in which recollection and anticipation are held in suspension.

## Acknowledgements

I would like to express my profound gratitude to Tadao Ando. At all times, during the ten years that it has taken to produce the photographs, I have been greeted with warmth and unequalled enthusiasm. The integrity of form, the harmony of light and colour, and the clarity of the architectural idea and its expression in the work of Ando have led me to a deeper understanding of the achievements of contemporary architecture.

Yumiko Ando also gave freely of her time, and offered assistance far beyond expectation. The access to all the buildings represented here was arranged with the utmost consideration. Tadao Ando also kindly allowed his original sketches to be reproduced.

In addition, I would like to express my gratitude to Mr and Mrs Hirotaka Kidosaki, for their support and commitment, and their generous invitations to photograph their house on several occasions. Many others have extended assistance, including the directors and staff of the public buildings, and the owners of private houses. I received kind assistance from Els Barents, Bokelberg, Eileen and John Harris, Jaap Lieverse, Iraklis Papaioannou and Karl Schawelka. I would like to thank Thomas Manss for the design of the book. I especially wish to express my gratitude to Phyllis Lambert, Director of the Canadian Centre for Architecture, Montreal, whose friendship and enthusiasm have been a constant source of encouragement.

# The Projects

## Atelier in Oyodo I

Formerly known as Tomishima House, this building was originally designed in 1972 for a family of four. Located in the centre of Osaka, it was situated on a narrow 47-square-metre strip of land, which was clipped off from one end of a wooden tenement house, built before the Second World War. A three-storey volume, its composition was organized around an atrium – a void – that spanned the height of the building. Sunlight penetrated this interior space through a skylight. However it was the quality rather than the quantity of light that was investigated here; the interior space interacted with the outside solely through the skylight, which illuminated each level of the house by means of the central atrium. Ten years after it was built, Tadao Ando bought the building and converted it into his studio. He enlarged it by expanding on to a neighbouring site and by adding to it in height.

**Tomishima House**

| | |
|---|---|
| Location | Osaka, Japan |
| Design period | January 1971–November 1971 |
| Construction period | February 1972–February 1973 |
| Structure | reinforced concrete |
| Site area | 55.2 m² |
| Building area | 36.2 m² |
| Total floor area | 72.4 m² |

**Atelier in Oyodo I**

| | |
|---|---|
| Design period | 1980, March 1981–September 1981 |
| Construction period | February 1981–March 1981 |
| | October 1981–February 1982, April 1986–May 1986 |
| Site area | 115.6 m² |
| Building area | 79.0 m² |
| Total floor area | 194.54 m² |

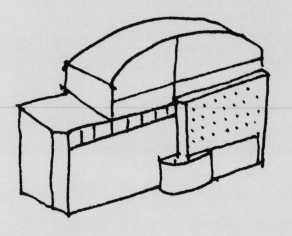

## Atelier in Oyodo II

The building has two floors below ground level and five above, the latter are penetrated by a five-storey atrium, or void, which gradually widens as it ascends. This stepped recessing of upper floors around the atrium lends dynamic variation to the interior space. Sunlight entering from a skylight reaches into the depths of the building. At times the atrium doubles as an impromptu 'lecture hall' with the speaker using the staircase as a podium. This introduction of an area with an irregular function renders the workplace a stimulating space, even when it is organized purely around the discharge of routine duties.

| | |
|---|---|
| Design period | June 1989–May 1990 |
| Construction period | June 1990–April 1991 |
| Structure | reinforced concrete |
| Site area | 115.6 m² |
| Building area | 91.7 m² |
| Total floor area | 451.7 m² |

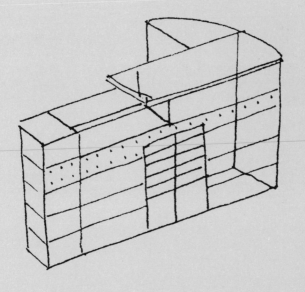

## Noguchi House

This house replaced an old wooden rowhouse in Osaka. Designed to create a world in miniature, it ensures three generations of the same family – grandparents, a young couple and their children – their privacy. A rectangular prism, 3.2 metres wide, 15 metres deep and three storeys high was inserted into the building, which was divided along its depth into three equal parts, the middle portion being transformed into a light-well. The house was also divided in two along its width, with one side given over to circulation spaces. The courtyard overlaps these circulation spaces and provides a buffer zone for the rooms inhabited by individual family members. Each room is arranged around the courtyard in various ways on three different levels.

Location ..................................................................................................................Osaka, Japan
Design period...................................................................................May 1985–September 1985
Construction period .....................................................................October 1985–May 1986
Structure.........................................................................................................reinforced concrete
Site area.........................................................................................................................68.5 m²
Building area .............................................................................................................40.0 m²
Total floor area .......................................................................................................106.3 m²

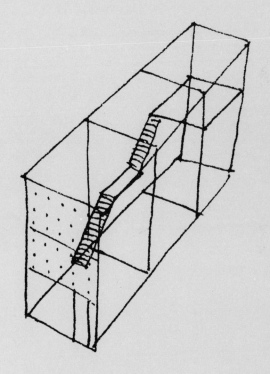

## Koshino House

Located on a densely wooded mountain slope, the Koshino House is set partly into the ground; its distinct geometric forms contrast powerfully with the irregular configuration of the land. The building consists of two parallel volumes, linked by an underground corridor, which define a central courtyard space. The shorter volume contains a double-height living room and the longer wing comprises a series of bedrooms. Though the later addition of the segment-shaped studio is parallel to the living-room volume, it enters into the composition as an opposing element contrasting with the earlier structures. Skylight bands and light slots allow sunlight to penetrate into all three volumes, creating delicate light sculptures on the interior walls.

| | |
|---|---|
| Location | Ashiya, Japan |
| Design period | September 1979–April 1980 |
| Construction period | August 1980–February 1981 |
| Structure | reinforced concrete |
| Site area | 1141.0 m² |
| Building area | 227.8 m² |
| Total floor area | 241.6 m² |

| Addition | |
|---|---|
| Location | Ashiya, Japan |
| Design period | January 1983–June 1983 |
| Construction period | November 1983–March 1984 |
| Structure | reinforced concrete |
| Site area | 1141.0 m² |
| Building area | 0 m² |
| Total floor area | 52.7 m² |

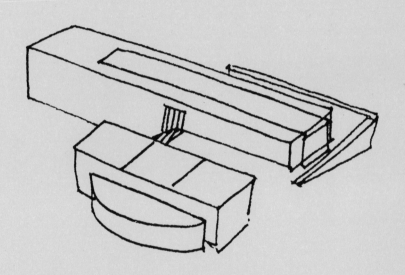

## Kidosaki House

Located in a quiet residential suburb, this house was built for a family of three generations – it accommodates a couple and their parents. Designed as a multi-dwelling unit, it affords the occupants privacy in their living quarters and companionship in their daily activities. The building consists of a cubic volume with a protective wall along the property line. The cubic volume's almost central position on the site endows the exterior spaces on the perimeter with a three-dimensional character. This arrangement creates a buffer zone around the lives of the families, while also providing a sense of communal territory.

| | |
|---|---|
| Location | Tokyo, Japan |
| Design period | October 1982–October 1985 |
| Construction period | October 1985–October 1986 |
| Structure | reinforced concrete |
| Site area | 610.9 m$^2$ |
| Building area | 351.5 m$^2$ |
| Total floor area | 556.1 m$^2$ |

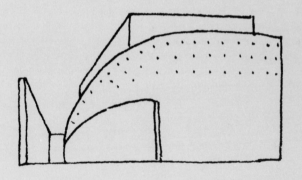

235

## Collezione

A commercial complex situated in a fashionable quarter of Tokyo, Collezione consists of two rectangular volumes spanned by a cube, an interlocking cylindrical volume and a protective perimeter wall, which inscribes an arc. In order to relate the building to the level of those surrounding it, half of its volume was located below ground level. The lower basement floor contains parking space, while the upper two basement floors house an exercise club and a swimming-pool. Boutiques occupy the ground and first floors, and the upper two floors accommodate showrooms, galleries and the owner's residence. A stepped plaza and a staircase, which spirals around the outer wall of the cylindrical volume, are placed at the centre of the building's composition.

Location................................................................................................Tokyo, Japan
Design period.............................................................March 1986–August 1987
Construction period.........................September 1987–September 1989
Structure ...........................................................steel and reinforced concrete
Site area..............................................................................................1683.5 m²
Building area.....................................................................................1175.3 m²
Total floor area ...............................................................................5709.7 m²

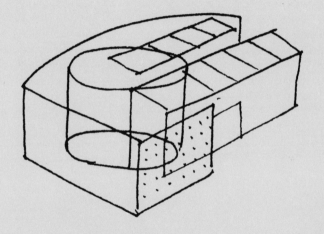

## Church of the Light

Located in a quiet residential suburb, this chapel derives its orientation from the direction of the sun and from the position of an adjacent church building. The church consists of a rectangular volume (a triple cube) sliced through at a 15-degree angle by a freestanding wall, which defines the chapel and its triangular entrance space. Entering through an opening in the angled wall, one has to turn 180 degrees to be aligned with the chapel. The floor descends in stages towards the altar, behind which is a wall penetrated by horizontal and vertical openings that form a crucifix. Both the floor and benches are made of low-cost wooden scaffolding planks, which, with their rough-textured surface, emphasize the simple and honest character of the space.

Location ........................................................................................................................................Ibaraki, Japan
Design period ...............................................................................................January 1987–May 1988
Construction period ..............................................................................................May 1988–April 1989
Structure .....................................................................................................................reinforced concrete
Site area ............................................................................................................................................838.6 m$^2$
Building area ...................................................................................................................................113.0 m$^2$
Total floor area ............................................................................................................................113.0 m$^2$

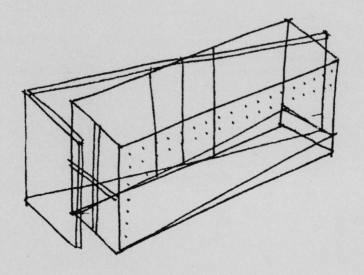

239

## Tent Tea House

Built on the roof of an old wooden house, the form of the Tent Tea House is evocative of a square balloon, which has softly landed on the top of the roof from the sky above. Its structure appears so small and fragile that it looks as if the slightest wind would carry it away. However, it is a space filled with intimate intention. Composed of steel supports, a glass floor and ceiling, it has a tent roof and screen, which can be rolled up and down to create a temporary space. The freedom of the Tent Tea House lies in the architect's choice of materials. From the outset, materials commonly used in traditional Japanese buildings were intentionally excluded. But the traditional Japanese module, 5 Shaku 8 Sun (175.4 cm), was adapted for the interior dimensions and for the height of the ceiling. It is this module for square space, alone, that endows the structure with a sense of tradition.

Location ......................................................................................................................................Osaka, Japan
Design period ................................................................................................................January 1987–April 1988
Construction period .................................................................................................................................April 1988
Structure .........................................................................................................................................................steel
Total floor area ..........................................................................................................................................3.3 m$^2$

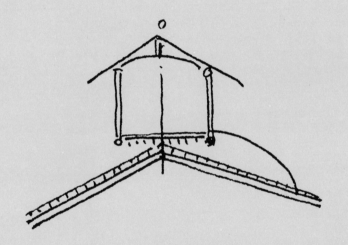

## Hata House

This house stands on a suburban hillside with a stream flowing nearby and the view of a national forest in the background. Its compositional arrangement is derived from the Japanese gardening technique *shakkei*, 'borrowed scenery'. Conceived as having two outlooks, part of the house is open and the other closed. The open part of the house faces south, that is in the direction of the national forest, and has an outdoor stepped terrace; on the top floor is a hall, paved with the same stone as the terrace; and on the ground floor is the hall, a multi-storey space, a dining room and a tatami room. From the dining room, one can see the green hillside beyond the terrace. On the ground floor, there is a bedroom facing a sunken court. This is the closed aspect of the house, where the landscape is shut out to allow one to sense more acutely nature in the guise of sunlight, wind and rain.

Location ................................................................................................................ Nishinomiya, Japan
Design period ........................................................................................ July 1983–February 1984
Construction period ........................................................................ March 1984–September 1984
Structure ........................................................................................................................ reinforced concrete
Site area .......................................................................................................................................... 441.5 m²
Building area ................................................................................................................................ 118.7 m²
Total floor area ........................................................................................................................ 207.2 m²

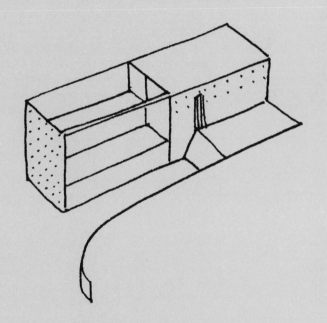

## Galleria Akka

Situated in a shopping area in the centre of Osaka, this retail/gallery structure is a rectilinear volume inserted among a chaotic array of low-rise commercial buildings, on a rectangular lot with a frontage of 8 metres and a depth of 40 metres. The tranquillity of the building's exterior suggests an intimate interior, yet once inside any expectations are immediately dashed by the central atrium – a vertically oriented space whose unconventional presence overwhelms the visitor. Stretching up five storeys from the basement, the atrium accounts for half of the building's volume. Facing the atrium is a curved wall with a 28-metre radius. A series of stairs climb the wall – ascending and descending flights of steps that pass each other on opposite sides of the wall. The unifying character of the curved, frosted-glass roof at the top of the atrium gives the building a strong architectural identity.

Location......................................................................................................................................Osaka, Japan
Design period ...............................................................................................October 1985–March 1987
Construction period ......................................................................................March 1987–April 1988
Structure.......................................................................................................................reinforced concrete
Site area ....................................................................................................................................324.2 m$^2$
Building area ...........................................................................................................................226.0 m$^2$
Total floor area ...................................................................................................................1027.1 m$^2$

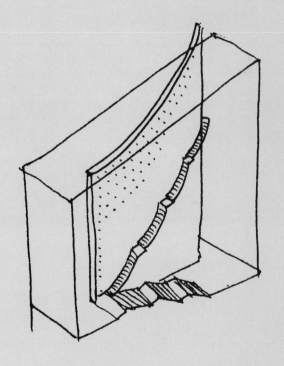

## Oxy Unagidani

This building is a commercial complex located in the main shopping area of central Osaka. It is composed of an L-shaped wall, which follows the property line, and a volume at a slight distance from the wall. The gap created between the wall and the building proper renders the building autonomous. All the shops and restaurants face on to this space, which also functions as a stairwell. The exterior wall of the main building is twisted at an angle of 12 degrees away from the L-shaped wall so as to draw people from the street into the shops. On the facade fronting the street, the building is glazed from floor to ceiling on all levels.

Location .................................................................................................................Minami, Osaka, Japan
Design period.....................................................................................................June 1986–October 1986
Construction period ...............................................................................November 1986–September 1987
Structure............................................................................................................................reinforced concrete
Site area .......................................................................................................................................193.6 m$^2$
Building area .............................................................................................................................123.8 m$^2$
Total floor area ........................................................................................................................472.9 m$^2$

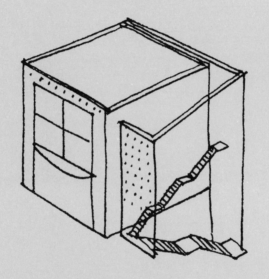

## Chapel on Mount Rokko

From its position on a verdant mountain slope, this small church enjoys a panoramic ocean view. The building consists of a chapel and bell-tower, a covered colonnade and a freestanding wall, which partially encloses the landscape. While the chapel is a concrete mass, the long colonnade is a glazed promenade. By turning right at the end of the colonnade, the visitor is led from a light-infused space into the dark chapel. The altar is directly ahead and, to the left of the altar, a large window – divided by a cross-shaped post and beam – frames the view of a green slope.

| | |
|---|---|
| Location | Kobe, Japan |
| Design period | January 1985–July 1985 |
| Construction period | August 1985–March 1986 |
| Structure | reinforced concrete |
| Site area | 7933.9 m² |
| Building area | 220.3 m² |
| Total floor area | 220.3 m² |

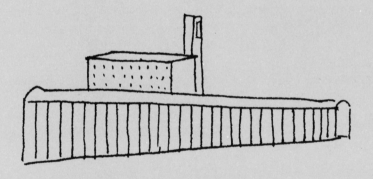

## Old/New Rokko Restaurant

The Old/New Restaurant complex's site is on a steep gradient of over 1:8, affording a distant view of the ocean. A multi-storey entrance hall separates, and at the same time brings into intimate proximity, the four eating areas, which include Japanese and Western restaurants. The whole building was composed around three aged camphor trees, which previously existed on the site. The perimeter retaining walls use the locally quarried granite stone that is a feature of traditional residences in this area.

Location...............................................................................................................Kobe, Japan
Design period.............................................................................January 1985–November 1985
Construction period............................................................December 1985–December 1986
Structure period.........................................................................................reinforced concrete
Site area.................................................................................................................1283.0 m²
Building area .............................................................................................................481.1 m²
Total floor area ..........................................................................................................806.5 m²

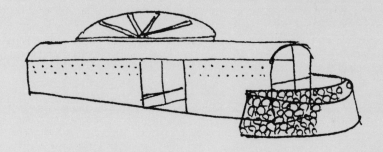

## Children's Museum

Situated on a hill overlooking a broad lake, the Museum is a cultural facility for the artistic education of children. It consists of three parts – the main museum, an intermediate plaza and a workshop complex – all linked by a long pathway marked by a series of walls, which dramatically slice through the slope of the hill. The main museum is a multi-functional complex, containing a library, indoor and outdoor theatres, exhibition gallery, multi-purpose hall and restaurant. It is composed of two staggered volumes, one of which connects with a fan-shaped building housing the theatres. A series of man-made pools surround the museum. The intermediate plaza is a walled external space, containing a grid of sixteen 9-metre -high columns. The workshop complex consists of a two-storey workshop building, square in plan, and set within a plaza.

Location ........................................................................................................................Himeji, Japan
Design period.......................................................................................March 1987–March 1988
Construction period..............................................................................March 1988–July 1989
Structure ..............................................................................................steel and reinforced concrete
Site area.............................................................................................................................87222.0 m²
Building area.........................................................................................................................3575.6 m²
Total floor area ...................................................................................................................7488.4 m²

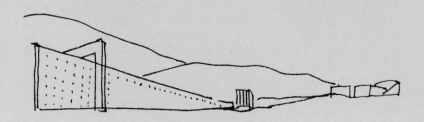

## RAIKA Headquarters Building

This office building, designed for a clothes manufacturer, is located in an area of reclaimed land that is being developed as the new hub of metropolitan Osaka. The lobby, the spacious atrium and the rooftop garden, are all conceived as functional spaces, which are attractive meeting places. The building is composed of several rectangular volumes arranged around a cylindrical form. There are three connected but distinct units, which are of a moderate height, and recede from the frontal thoroughfare. Trees, planted along the perimeter of the site, partially screen the building and subdue its presence in the immediate environment. A public plaza has been created at the south-west corner of the site, adjacent to a building containing shops, an exhibition hall and training facilities, with galleries on the upper levels and parking in the basement. Within the seven-storey cylindrical atrium of the main building, a ramp ascends, silhouetted against the arc of the glass-block curtain wall.

Location ....................................................................................................................... Osaka, Japan
Design period ................................................................................... June 1986–December 1987
Construction period ................................................................. December 1987–December 1989
Structure ............................................................................................ steel and reinforced concrete
Site area ....................................................................................................................... 23487.8 m$^2$
Building area ................................................................................................................. 9771.4 m$^2$
Total floor area ........................................................................................................... 42791.8 m$^2$

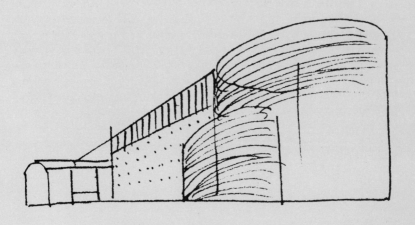

## Museum of Literature

The Museum of Literature is located on a lush green hill about 500 metres from Himeji Castle, which is a national treasure and a historic landmark, in the centre of Himeji. The design of the building consciously reflects its vicinity to the castle. Mainly devoted to the philosopher Tetsurou Watsuji (1889–1960), the museum displays exhibits related to him. There are three floors above ground level and a basement, which houses exhibition space and a lecture hall. The building is composed of two cubic volumes, with ground plans of 22.5 metres square overlapping at a 30-degree angle. A cylinder with a 20-metre radius, housing the exhibition space, encompasses one of the cubes, forming a three-level atrium. Water cascades and ramps wrap around the exterior of the building, and Himeji Castle can be viewed in the distance on approaching the museum.

Location .................................................................................................................................Himeji, Japan
Design period.................................................................................................................July 1988–July 1989
Construction period................................................................................................July 1989–March 1991
Structure ...............................................................................................steel and reinforced concrete
Site area .............................................................................................................................15600.9 m$^2$
Building area ...................................................................................................................1324.1 m$^2$
Total floor area ............................................................................................................3814.5 m$^2$

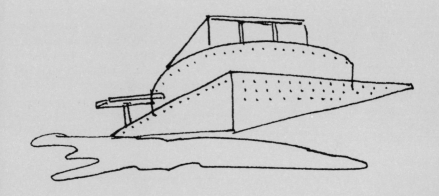

## Church on the Water

Located on a plain in the depths of the province of Hokkaido, this church has a plan of two overlapping squares of different sizes. The building faces towards a shallow artificial lake, created by the diversion of a nearby stream. A freestanding, L-shaped wall extends along one side of the lake and wraps around the back of the church. A gentle slope, overlooking the lake, ascends alongside the wall, leading to the top of the smaller volume where, within a glass-enclosed space open to the sky, four large crosses are arranged in a square formation, their transverse arms almost touching. From this point, the visitor descends a darkened stairway to emerge into the rear of the chapel. The wall behind the altar is fully glazed, providing a panorama of the lake, in which the large crucifix is seen rising from the surface of the water. This wall can be slid entirely to one side, directly opening the interior of the church up to the natural surroundings.

| | |
|---|---|
| Location | Hokkaido, Japan |
| Design period | September 1985–April 1988 |
| Construction period | April 1988–September 1988 |
| Structure | reinforced concrete |
| Site area | 6730.0 m² |
| Building area | 344.9 m² |
| Total floor area | 520.0 m² |

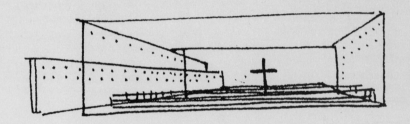

## Forest of Tombs Museum

This museum is dedicated to preserving and promoting an understanding of the historic cultural legacy of the Iwabari burial mounds in Northern Kumamoto Prefecture. In order not to intrude on the site any more than was necessary, it was designed as a raised platform from which the tombs and their surroundings can be viewed, and half of its volume was buried below ground. Visitors approach the museum on foot, passing first through a lush green forest. Though 250 metres away from the famed Futago-zuka, a large keyhole-shaped tumulus, the museum is positioned symmetrically to it. This engenders the perception of the museum as a contemporary tumulus. The building consists of a rectangular volume that is 26 x 79.2 metres; a circular courtyard, which is 15.8 metres in radius; and an L-shaped wall that penetrates to the centre of the circular courtyard. The excavation grounds lie just beyond the wall of the circular courtyard, while inside a ramp winds around the wall, leading visitors through displays of artefacts.

| | |
|---|---|
| Location | Kumamoto, Japan |
| Design period | December 1989–June 1990 |
| Construction period | October 1990–March 1992 |
| Structure | steel and reinforced concrete |
| Site area | 6338.0 m² |
| Building area | 1448.8 m² |
| Total floor area | 2099.0 m² |

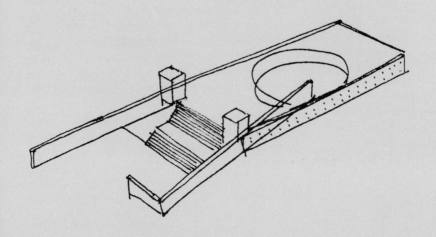

261

## Naoshima Contemporary Art Museum

The site is on the bluff of a slender cape on Naoshima Island's southern tip, overlooking the quiet surf on the beach below. The design of the museum is oriented to receive visitors directly by boat. Landing on a wharf, visitors are greeted by a stepped plaza that functions as the museum entrance, but also houses a museum annex underground and doubles as a stage for outdoor performances. It is only after climbing the plaza steps that the stone-rubble walls of the main museum come into view. More than half of the building's volume sits underground so as not to intrude on the scenic surroundings. Visitors ascend the slope, pass through the main building's entrance and then are led into the gallery – a large underground volume two-levels high, 50 metres long, and 8 metres wide. The hotel building, gallery and stepped terrace are all opened up to the ocean, and each draws within its interior spaces the tranquil ocean scenery of commuting boats and setting sun. This architecture, established amid the vastness of nature, functions as an earthwork creating a new landscape.

Location ......................................................................................................................Naoshima, Japan
Design period..............................................................................................May 1988–September 1990
Construction period ...............................................................................October 1990–April 1992
Structure.........................................................................................................................reinforced concrete
Site area ..............................................................................................................................44700.0 m²
Building area ....................................................................................................................1775.5 m²
Total floor area ...............................................................................................................3643.4 m²

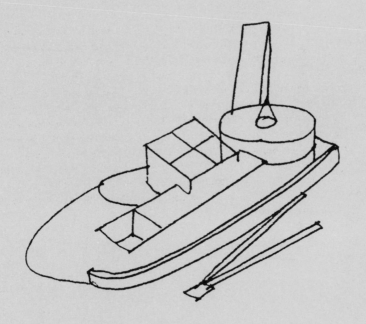

## Rokko Housing II

Located on a site adjacent to Rokko Housing I, this housing complex shares the same 60-degree slope as its neighbouring block, but has an area nearly four times as large. The building is founded on a uniform grid of 5.2 x 5.2 metres, and consists of three connected, but distinct clusters of dwellings, each five-units square. Adapting the uniform grid to the steepness of the slope generates asymmetry in plan and section – introducing complexity into the consistency of the geometry and producing a dynamic architectural order. The resulting symmetry also endows the entire complex with eastern light. The building is composed axially around the line of a central staircase, which shifts at the intermediate level, where it links with approaches to each cluster. A north/south gap divides each cluster, providing communal space and resolving requirements for lighting and ventilation. Within the overall geometric uniformity of the complex, each of the fifty dwellings is unique in size and format.

| | |
|---|---|
| Location | Kobe, Japan |
| Design period | August 1985–May 1989 |
| Construction period | June 1989–May 1993 |
| Structure | steel and reinforced concrete |
| Site area | 5998.1 m² |
| Building area | 2964.7 m² |
| Total floor area | 9043.6 m² |

## Chikatsu-Asuka Historical Museum

The Chikatsu-Asuka Historical Museum is dedicated to exhibiting and researching *kofun* (burial mound) culture. Unlike conventional museums, this building not only exhibits the excavated objects, but acts as a place from which the tombs themselves can be viewed in their surroundings. The building, sited in a basin, was conceived as a hill from which to view the entire excavation area. Its roof, which is in effect a large stepped plaza, is used for various performances and events, and the entire facility and its grounds are designed to function as a recreational hub for the region. Inside the museum, the display areas are dark, as the objects are exhibited as they were found in the tombs. Visitors experience the sensation that they are entering an actual tomb.

| | |
|---|---|
| Location | Osaka, Japan |
| Design period | April 1990–November 1991 |
| Construction period | December 1991–March 1994 |
| Structure | steel and reinforced concrete |
| Site area | 14318.3 m² |
| Building area | 3407.8 m² |
| Total floor area | 5925.2 m² |

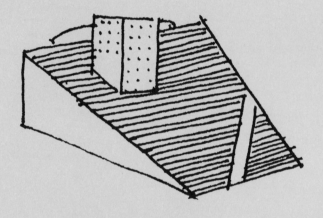

## Vitra Seminar House

This guest house was designed for use by the executive personnel of a furniture company, and is located near the company's production base in Germany. As it is on a flat site the height of the building is minimized by situating part of the volume underground. It is composed of three elements: a rectangular volume running parallel to the walls of the square sunken court; another rectangular volume, which penetrates the court at a 60-degree angle; and a cylindrical volume that forms a spatial void and interlocks with two rectilinear volumes. The building has two levels, accommodating conference rooms, a library, private rooms, and a lobby – all of which open onto the sunken court.

Location ........................................................................................................ Weil-am-Rhein, Germany
Design period ............................................................................................. January 1989–May 1992
Construction period .................................................................................... June 1992–July 1993
Structure ............................................................................................................ reinforced concrete
Site area ..................................................................................................................... 19408.0 m²
Building area .............................................................................................................. 360.9 m²
Total floor area ........................................................................................................... 508.3 m²

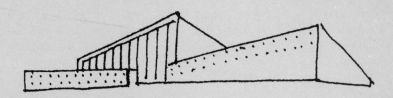

## Water Temple

A hill on Awaji Island, which affords a sweeping view of Osaka Bay, is the location for Hompukuji, the Water Temple, a new main temple for the Shingon Buddhist sect. The temple hall is placed below ground, beneath a large oval pond filled with green lotus plants. The hall is entered by means of a descending staircase, which divides the pond, appearing to draw visitors under water. The hall is composed of a round room, gridded with timber pillars, which is contained within a square enclosure. The interior of the hall and its pillars are stained vermilion; this traditional Buddhist colour becomes intense at sunset when the reddish glow of twilight suffuses the space, casting long shadows from the pillars deep inside the subterranean space. The design of the temple creates a sequence of experiences that transcends everyday life.

| | |
|---|---|
| Location | Awaji-shima, Japan |
| Design period | November 1989–December 1990 |
| Construction period | November 1990–September 1991 |
| Structure | reinforced concrete |
| Site area | 2990.8 m² |
| Building area | 859.5 m² |
| Total floor area | 417.2 m² |

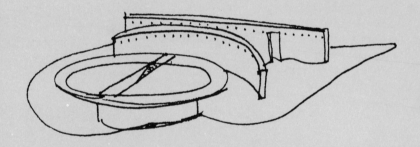

# Nariwa Museum

Nariwacho, a provincial town in Okayama Prefecture, is located to the north of the city of Kurasbiki. For many years it has enjoyed economic prosperity because of the copper mines in the area. It is also well known for folkhouses called 'fukiya' that are coloured a distinctive red ochre. The museum is located between the site of an old fukiya residence surrounded by a stone wall and a steep slope to the south. The design of this museum creates another wall layer with a concrete box inside it. Visitors approaching the museum first encounter the old stone wall, that has witnessed the passage of time, and then ascend an angled ramp around the concrete box and get a visual tour of the west-facing planted slope, where a large expanse of water intervenes between the slope and the museum. The museum thus becomes a place where nature, culture and history come together.

Location ............................................................................................................ Nariwa, Okayama, Japan
Design period ................................................................................................................ July 1992–March 1993
Construction period ................................................................................................ April 1993–October 1994
Structure ........................................................................................................................................ reinforced concrete
Site area ............................................................................................................................................................ 7194 m²
Building area .................................................................................................................................................. 1490 m²
Total floor area ............................................................................................................................................ 2646 m²

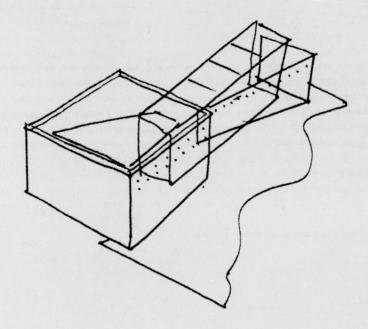

273

## Naoshima Contemporary Art Museum Annexe

Located on top of the hill behind the site of the existing art museum and hotel complex, which was completed in 1992, this project provides an extension to the hotel and includes multiple spaces for use as a gallery. This annexe, located 40 metres above the lower buildings, is accessed by riding a small cable car. Built as a single-storey building with an oval plan, it becomes a base point for the greening of the whole hill with a wide variety of trees and flora. The building, most of it buried into the hill, occupies an oval plane with a 40-metre major axis and 30-metre minor axis. The centre is designed as a water garden surrounded by a colonnade which can be used as a semi-outdoor gallery. A cascade of water decorates the entrance and a green garden was placed between the boundaries of the oval and the square perimeter. The water appears to drop directly into the ocean, and the garden forms a continuation of the backdrop provided by the surrounding greenery, extending a roof-top garden, and facing and opening towards the sea.

| | |
|---|---|
| Location | Naoshima, Kagawa, Japan |
| Design period | August 1993–September 1994 |
| Construction period | October 1994–July 1995 |
| Structure | reinforced concrete |
| Site area | 53.368 m² |
| Building area | 693 m² |
| Total floor area | 598 m² |

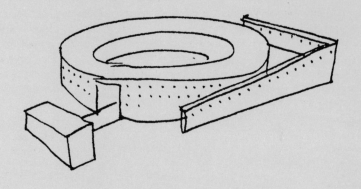

## FABRICA, Benetton Research Centre

A seventeenth-century Palladian villa provides the location for a new research centre at Treviso, near Venice, in Italy. The restoration of the villa was the starting point for the design of this new institution that accepts young students from around the world to study photography, graphics and textiles. The facilities include study rooms, studios, a restaurant and library. All these rooms face the plaza and interconnect with it; the plaza is thus a place that accommodates a variety of social and spatial interactions. A new gallery, 7 metres wide, penetrates the old building, and its colonnade extends across a pond in front of the villa. By adding new architecture, the design seeks to enhance the old villa's charm and vitality, and to induce a dynamic relationship between old and new that can transcend time.

| | |
|---|---|
| Location | Villorba, Treviso, Italy |
| Design period | April 1992–October 1995 |
| Construction period | January 1993–October 1996 |
| Structure | reinforced concrete |
| Site area | 51000 m² |
| Building area | 1250 m² |
| Total floor area | 11000 m² |

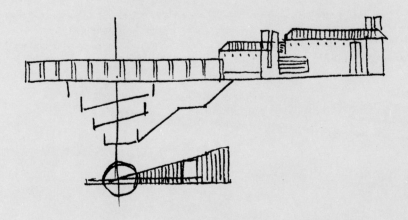

## Meditation Space, UNESCO

This small 'meditation space' was built alongside the UNESCO Headquarters in Paris in commemoration of its fiftieth anniversary. This space is intended to be a place of prayer for eternal, global peace for all peoples of the world, transcending their religious, ethnic, cultural and historical differences and conflicts. The meditation space is a single-storey, reinforced concrete structure, 6.5 metres in height. It has a serene, solemn appearance in keeping with its name. With the cooperation of the city of Hiroshima, granite which was exposed to radiation from the atomic bomb is used for the floor and the base of the artificial pond to symbolize the quest for eternal peace on earth.

| | |
|---|---|
| Location | Paris, France |
| Design period | January 1994–May 1995 |
| Construction period | April 1995–October 1995 |
| Structure | reinforced concrete |
| Site area | 350 m² |
| Building area | 33 m² |
| Total floor area | 33 m² |

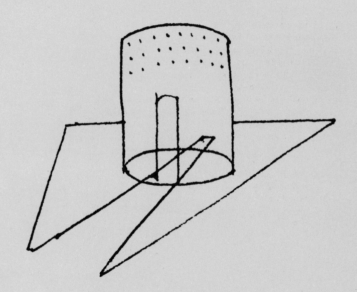

279

All works in Japan unless otherwise stated

| | |
|---|---|
| 1973 | Tomishima House, Oyodo Ward, Osaka |
| 1974 | Tatsumi House, Taisho Ward, Osaka |
| | Shibata House, Ashiya, Hyogo |
| 1975 | Soseikan (Yamaguchi House), Takarazuka, Hyogo |
| 1976 | Row House, Sumiyoshi (Azuma House), Osaka |
| | Hirabayashi House, Suita, Osaka |
| | Bansho House, Nishi-Kamo, Aichi |
| | Tezukayama Tower Plaza (commercial and residential complex), Sumiyoshi Ward, Osaka |
| | Okamoto Housing, Higashinada Ward, Kobe (project) |
| 1976–77 | Art Gallery Complex (project) |
| 1977 | Tezukayama House, Abeno Ward, Osaka |
| | Matsumoto House, Ashiya, Hyogo |
| 1978 | Ishihara House, Ikuno Ward, Osaka |
| | Okusu House, Setagaya Ward, Tokyo |
| 1979 | Horiuchi House, Sumiyoshi Ward, Osaka |
| | Matsutani House, Fushimi Ward, Kyoto |
| | Ohnishi House, Sumiyoshi Ward, Osaka |
| | Ueda House, Soja, Okayama |

| | |
|---|---|
| 1980 | Step Commercial Complex, Takamatsu, Kagawa |
| | Matsumoto House, Wakayama, Wakayama |
| 1981 | Koshino House, Ashiya, Hyogo |
| | Kojima Housing, Kurashiki, Okayama |
| | Atelier in Oyodo I, Oyodo Ward, Osaka |
| | Bansho House extensions, Nishi-Kamo, Aichi |
| 1982 | Atelier in Oyodo Extension, Oyodo Ward, Osaka |
| | Izutsu (townhouse in Kujo), Nishi Ward, Osaka |
| | Ishii House, Hamamatsu, Shizuoka Prefecture, |
| | BIGI Atelier, Shibuya Ward, Tokyo |
| | Soseikan Tea House, Takarazuka, Hyogo |
| | Akabane House, Setagaya Ward, Tokyo |
| 1983 | Umemiya House, Tarumi Ward, Kobe |
| | Rokko Housing I, Nada Ward, Kobe |
| | Kaneko House, Shibuya Ward, Tokyo |

| | |
|---|---|
| 1984 | Motegi House, Nagata Ward, Kobe |
| | Koshino House extension, Ashiya, Hyogo |
| | Iwasa House, Ashiya, Hyogo Prefecture |
| | Festival, Naha, Okinawa Prefecture |
| | Time's I, Nakagyo Ward, Kyoto |
| | Hata House, Nishinomiya, Hyogo |
| 1985 | Atelier Yoshie Inaba, Shibuya Ward, Tokyo |
| | Nakayama House, Nara, Nara Prefecture |
| | Noguchi House, Osaka |
| 1986 | Chapel on Mount Rokko, Kobe |
| | Old/New Rokko Restaurant, Kobe |
| | Kidosaki House, Setagaya Ward, Tokyo |
| 1987 | Oxy Unagidani, Minami, Osaka |
| 1988 | Galleria Akka, Chuo Ward, Osaka |
| | Church on the Water, Tomamu, Hokkaido |
| | Tent Tea House, Tea House, Osaka |
| 1989 | Church of the Light, Ibaraki, Osaka |
| | Children's Museum, Hyogo, Himeji, Hyogo |
| | RAIKA Headquarter's Building, Suminoe Ward, Osaka |
| | Collezione, Tokyo |

TADAO ANDO: THE COLOURS OF LIGHT is the result of ten years' collaboration between English photographer Richard Pare and internationally renowned Japanese architect Tadao Ando. This book includes a unique insight into twenty-seven Ando works, including such buildings as the Kidosaki House, the Church on the Water, the Naoshima Contemporary Art Museum and the Meditation Space for UNESCO. The photographic portfolio is complemented by an essay by Tom Heneghan and sketches by Tadao Ando, which accompany the project texts at the back of the book. *The Colours of Light* was published in 1996 to critical acclaim, and now for the first time it is available as a miniature edition.

RICHARD PARE received his MFA in photography in 1973 from the Art Institute of Chicago. He is currently the consulting curator of photography for the Canadian Centre for Architecture and has exhibited at the Art Institute of Chicago and the Museum of Modern Art and Max Protetch Gallery in New York.

TOM HENEGHAN was educated at the Architectural Association School of Architecture, where he taught from 1979. In 1990, he was invited by Arata Isozaki to participate in the 'Kumamoto Art Polis' programme in Japan and established his Tokyo office. He is currently professor at Kogakuin University in Tokyo.

ISBN 0-7148-3999-X

9 780714 839998